Marriage Matters

Tony Evans

MOODY PUBLISHERS
CHICAGO

Editor: Christopher Reese
Interior Design: Ragont Design
Cover Design: Smartt Guys design
Cover Image: Nattthawat Wongrat / 123RF

Library of Congress Cataloging-in-Publication Data

Evans, Tony, 1949-
Marriage matters / Tony Evans.
    p. cm.
ISBN 978-0-8024-2325-2
1. Spouses--Religious life. 2. Marriage--Religious aspects--Christianity.
I. Title.
 BV4596.M3E92 2010
 241'.63--dc22

                            2010007623

CONTENTS

TRANSCENDENCE: THE ORIGIN OF MARRIAGE

For far too many people, the subject of marriage is like a three-ring circus. First, there is the engagement ring. Next comes the wedding ring. Then, there is suffering.

One lady said that she got married because she was looking for the ideal but it quickly turned into an ordeal, and now she wants a new deal. One man said that he and his wife were happy for twenty years . . . and then they got married.

Many people today are disappointed with marriage. They wake up one morning only to discover that the reality they live in looms far from what they had once dreamt or imagined. Because of this, some are getting out of marriage almost as quickly as they got into it.

On top of that, the breakup of a marriage these days

doesn't seem to carry the same gravity that it did in the past. So-called "no-fault" divorces offer the option of an amicable split. My question is, if things are so amicable, then why not stay married? What we are experiencing today is the ending of marriages without even a hint of remorse.

It reminds me of a guy who went to the Super Bowl. The stadium was packed, but the seat next to him sat empty. The man behind him questioned him about the empty seat. He answered, "That seat was for my wife. She would have been here, but she died."

The other man offered his condolences and asked him if he didn't have a friend that he could have asked to come with him rather than let the seat remain empty. The man replied, "I do, but all my friends said they wanted to go to the funeral instead."

Now, I realize I'm making light of a weighty subject, but I'm doing so to illustrate how the seriousness of the wedding vows seems to no longer be honored. Statistics remind us what we already know, either from personal experience or from our friends, and that is that over 50 percent of all marriages will end in divorce. Over half of every promise made that "until death do us part" gets broken.

Because of this, what I would like to examine is the nature of the agreement we make when we get married. If we do not understand this agreement, then we will not be prone to protect it. What's even worse is that neither will we be apt to benefit from it.

One day a boy lost one of his contact lenses. He spent a significant amount of time trying to locate it, but he couldn't. Eventually, he told his mom. The boy's mom began looking for the contact lens with him and found it in only a matter of minutes. The boy asked, "How could you find that contact lens in just a few minutes when I must have looked for twenty minutes?"

The mom said, "That's easy. You didn't find it because you were looking for a contact lens. I found it because I was looking for $250."

It all depends on how you view it.

Our marriages today are deteriorating at such a high rate not because we no longer get along, but because we have lost sight of the purpose and prosperity of the marriage covenant.

Most people today view marriage as a means of looking for love, happiness, and fulfillment. Make no mistake about it, those things are important. Those things are critical. They are just not the most important, or the most critical. Yet because we have made second things first, as important as second things are, we are having trouble finding anything at all.

Before we conclude our time together in this marriage guide, I want you to view marriage from a different perspective. I want you to see it differently.

Marriage is a covenant. It is a covenantal union designed to strengthen the capability of each partner to carry out the plan of God in their lives. Marriage matters.

GOD'S DESCRIPTION OF MARRIAGE

Let's begin by looking at Malachi. In the book of Malachi, God is complaining against His people because they have wandered away from Him. They have taken a detour from God's plan for their lives.

One of God's complaints is found in chapter 2, verses 13 and 14. We read,

> This is another thing you do: you cover the altar of the Lord with tears, with weeping and with groaning, because He no longer regards the offering or accepts it with favor from your hand. Yet you say, "For what reason?" Because the Lord has been a witness between you and the wife of your youth, against whom you have dealt treacherously, though she is your companion and your wife by covenant.

Did you catch that? The passage specifically identifies marriage as a "covenant." The term "covenant" used to be regularly attached to the concept of marriage. The word has gotten lost in our contemporary language, but it is the biblical description of marriage used throughout Scripture.

The problems come when we don't realize that marriage *is* a covenant, nor do we know what a covenant is. Because if we do not know what a covenant is, then we do not know what we are supposed to have, develop, or protect over time. It's like trying to hit a bull's-eye without a target.

For most people, a covenant is simply some sort of

formal contractual arrangement. While this is true about the nature of a covenant, a covenant is also much more than that. In the Bible, a covenant is a spiritually binding relationship between God and His people inclusive of certain agreements, conditions, benefits, and effects.

> # MARRIAGE IS A COVENANTAL UNION DESIGNED TO STRENGTHEN THE CAPABILITY OF EACH PARTNER TO CARRY OUT THE PLAN OF GOD IN THEIR LIVES.

Whenever God wanted to formalize His relationship with His people, He would establish a covenant. There are a number of these agreements in the Bible such as the Abrahamic covenant, the Mosaic covenant, the Davidic covenant, and the new covenant. These are formal arrangements that are spiritually binding in a legal capacity between God and His people.

Marriage is another form of a covenant that God has established.

What we are going to do throughout this and the remaining chapters is to delve deeper into the purpose and

practical aspects of marriage, as well as the three fundamental facets that make up a covenant: transcendence, hierarchy, and ethics.

If you can grab, own, and apply these truths in your
life, you will have a God-centered perspective on marriage that can impact not only the rest of your life but future generations to come.

FIRST COVENANT FACET: TRANSCENDENCE

The first facet of a covenant is a big theological word
called *transcendence*. (We'll cover the other two facets, hierarchy and ethics, in later chapters.) Transcendence simply means that God is in charge. Covenants are both
initiated and ruled by God.

Now, that might seem like an obvious statement and
one that we don't need to spend too much time on, but
transcendence is a key principle in a covenant. In order for
a covenant to successfully function, carrying with it both
the benefits and security that a covenant supplies, it has to
be set up according to God's expectations and regulations.

Covenants can never operate without the ongoing
involvement of God. Biblical, spiritual, and theological
covenants assume God's integration into every aspect of the
covenantal relationship in order for that covenant to work.

When the practical realities of God are dismissed from
the marital covenantal relationship, it becomes an invitation
to the Devil to create havoc in the home. This happens because there has been a departure from transcendence.

Since God is ultimately in charge of the covenant of marriage, the first place to look to gain insight into the makings of a purposeful marriage is God's viewpoint on marriage.

GOD'S PERSPECTIVE ON MARRIAGE

Most people learn about marriage from an illegitimate source. They learn about marriage from the television, their friends, or the home that they grew up in. If you grew up in a functioning home, then that would be fine. But many did not, so the home—along with the media and friends—often merge together to form a distorted perspective on the covenant of marriage.

Without a divine frame of reference, we will stray from God's formula for a healthy, productive relationship. What is this divine frame of reference? God, as far back as in the garden of Eden, gave us His perspective through the very first marriage.

One of the rules of studying the Bible is called the Law of First Mention. The Law of First Mention simply states that if you want to see what God says about a matter, look at the first time He brings it up. You do this because the first time He brings it up will typically tell you how He thinks about it. Everything else will build on that first time. While it may add to it or expand it, it doesn't cancel out His first mention unless He says that it does at a later point.

Marriage starts off in the book of Genesis. Before

there was sin, there was marriage. Marriage was put in a sinless environment created by God. It was put there for a purpose, which we will discover as we dig deeper into the opening chapters.

"LET THEM RULE"

Looking at the book of Genesis in chapter 1, we read that God has been very active creating many different things. He has created the heavens and the earth in such a way that they are functional, vibrant, and pulsating with life.

On the fifth day, God formed the creatures that would live upon the earth. Then on the sixth day, He came to the paramount of His creation purposes—the creation of mankind.

Let's look at a few verses in Genesis chapter 1. We read,

> Then God said, "Let Us make man in Our image, according to Our likeness; and let them rule over the fish of the sea and over the birds of the sky and over the cattle and over all the earth, and over every creeping thing that creeps on the earth." God created man in His own image, in the image of God He created him; male and female He created them. God blessed them; and God said to them, "Be fruitful and multiply, and fill the earth, and subdue it; and rule over the fish of the sea and over the birds of the sky and over every living thing that moves on the earth." (Genesis 1:26–28)

Notice that in verse 26, we read that "God said . . ."

In verse 27, we see that "God created . . ."

And in verse 28, we find that "God blessed . . ." God said it. God created it. Then, God blessed it. Don't lose sight of that because it demonstrates that the issuance of the marriage covenant comes directly from God. That is an integral point to remember, as you will see later on.

> # WITHOUT A DIVINE FRAME OF REFERENCE, WE WILL STRAY FROM GOD'S FORMULA FOR A HEALTHY, PRODUCTIVE RELATIONSHIP.

The first thing God said was that mankind will be made in "Our image according to Our likeness; and let them rule . . ." Be careful not to skim over that too quickly because what we have just read is a staggering statement. It is a statement that stretches beyond comprehension, yet it is often so easily missed.

Here we have God creating man, male and female, and after doing so, He gives them a common goal. He says your common goal is to exercise dominion over the world in which I have placed you.

God says that mankind will mirror His image on earth, but then He says that there will be more than that for them. He is going to "let them rule." He is going to let humanity exercise dominion and authority.

What we see in verse 26 is God delegating to mankind the full responsibility for managing His earthly creation. God decides to indirectly control the affairs of earth by letting mankind exercise direct dominion. He has placed an agent on earth to serve as His representative to carry out in history His desires from eternity.

Not only does God proffer the delegation to rule, He also grants the freedom to rule, the responsibility to rule, and the right to rule on His behalf as owner. But what He does not do, please notice, is *force* man to rule. He says, "Let them rule." He does not say He is going to *make* them rule.

What that means is that you can have a happy marriage or a miserable marriage depending on whether your rule is reflecting His image. God isn't going to make you rule. He isn't going to make you have a happy marriage. He sets up the fundamentals of a covenant, and gives you the option of utilizing them.

Oftentimes, the well-being of the home is determined by whether the man is reflecting God's image in his role, or the woman is reflecting Him in her role. Once that mirror gets broken, the reflection that is supposed to happen in the relationship gets broken with it. Virtually every time there is a marital breakdown, it is because one or both parties are functioning outside of the covenantal fundamental of transcendence. They are functioning with a broken mirror.

God says, "I am in charge. I have made man in My own image. And now I am letting him call the shots within the parameters I have declared." That is my contemporary Evans translation of this passage in Genesis.

But don't confuse what God is saying. God is not giving up ownership of anything by relegating rulership. Psalm 24 tells us plainly, "The earth is the Lord's, and all it contains, the world, and those who dwell in it" (Psalm 24:1). God still claims ownership. But while He claims ownership, He also grants freedom.

This truth explains a lot of things that people often ask about. Things like, "If God *is* God, then how did this terrible thing happen?" Or, "Why did that bad thing happen?" Or, "How is there chaos if God is a God of order?"

Things happen and there is chaos because God has said, "Let them rule." God has given man the freedom, and responsibility, to rule—for good or for bad, for yes or for no, and for positive or for negative impact.

What Satan tries to get us to do is to either relinquish our rule by handing it over to him through deceiving us into believing that he has authority, or he tries to get us to rule poorly based on our own judgments and distorted views. It isn't until we rule with wisdom under the transcendence of God that we will become the rulers He intended. It is then that we enter into the complete realization of God's design for our lives.

PARAMETERS FOR RULING

God reigns over all, but He has delegated dominion at this unique juncture in history when mankind lives on the earth. We see this in the book of Psalms. Psalm 115 says, "The heavens are the heavens of the Lord, but the earth He has given to the sons of men" (vs.16).

What this means is that God has decided to respect your decisions, and that much of His action will be determined by your action. Most people are sitting around waiting on God to act, but God is often waiting on man to act. While He has maintained a base of sovereign boundaries, a sphere He will not allow men to trespass on, He has simultaneously opened up a field where we get to call the plays, leaving Him to respond accordingly.

He has not relinquished His sovereignty, but He has given us an enormous slice of dominion.

EAT FREELY

Leaving chapter 1 and moving into chapter 2 of Genesis, we discover more about this rule: "The Lord God commanded the man, saying, 'From any tree of the garden you may eat freely; but from the tree of the knowledge of good and evil you shall not eat, for in the day that you eat from it you will surely die" (Genesis 2:16–17).

I want you to notice what God says we *can* have in this passage first. God says that from "any tree of the garden" we may freely eat. What we often do, and what legalism often does, is look at that passage, or passages similar to it, and focuses on the thing that we cannot have. We do this all the while ignoring the hundreds of things God has just told us are free for us to enjoy.

> # GOD REIGNS OVER ALL, BUT HE HAS DELEGATED DOMINION AT THIS UNIQUE JUNCTURE IN HISTORY WHEN MANKIND LIVES ON THE EARTH.

Whenever our list of "can't haves" or "can't do's" exceeds our list of what we are free to do, then we have gone far beyond what Scripture is saying. The essence of the Christian life should be measured by what you get to enjoy, not by what you are denied.

God says, "From any tree of the garden you may eat freely; but from the tree of the knowledge of good and evil you shall not eat . . ." In other words, you are free to enjoy everything God has to offer you, other than the one thing that will open up to you the opportunity to determine for yourself what is good or bad, right or wrong. That rule is not an option. We are to live by divine revelation rather than human inclination. This was the limitation put on mankind not only to protect and guide us, but also to remind us of our subordination underneath God.

KEEPING THE GARDEN

This brings us to a staggering reality about marriage whose implications are far beyond what you might have expected. We looked earlier at Genesis chapter 1 where we saw that God made man in His own image. Chapter 2, as we will discover, comes back around to tell us how God did it, what He did, and why He did it. Chapter 2 explains the details of the summary given in chapter 1.

God has made a garden. He has made a unique place of service, and He has given Adam a unique calling within that sphere. Unlike the animals, which God created in groups, God didn't create man that way. He created man in a distinct process for a distinct reason.

We read about this process in chapter 2: "Then the Lord God said, 'It is not good for the man to be alone; I will make him a helper suitable for him'" (Genesis 2:18). The first thing I want us to note from that passage is that it is God who is giving the directive. We don't hear Adam complaining. Adam isn't saying, "Oh no, I'm twenty-five and I'm not married yet. Why don't you send someone to help me! I'm so alone!"

No, up until then Adam has been functioning as a successful single. What makes him so content and satisfied? He is content because he has been fulfilling his calling. He has been operating in his garden. He has been doing what he was created to do within the sphere God had created for him.

Please notice that before God ever made a woman, He made Adam and gave him a job. The first thing He did was tell Adam to go to work. This way, Adam knew responsibility under God before he was given responsibility over a woman.

When a man has not learned responsibility under God—men, I'm talking to you right now—he will be irresponsible concerning the one he is placed over. When a woman then comes underneath an irresponsible man, she has opened herself up to a very frustrating life. That is why the very first thing God did when He created Adam was to give Adam a calling and a responsibility.

We read in verse 15, "Then the Lord God took the man and put him into the garden of Eden to cultivate it and keep it." The Hebrew word for "keep" is our English word meaning "to guard" or "protect." Adam was to guard and protect the garden. That was where his home would be. And that was what he would oversee.

The question we need to ask is, From what was Adam to guard and protect the garden? This is a perfect world. Not quite, actually. This is a sinless environment, but there is a serpent already there who is going to show up again in chapter 3. The Devil is already there.

Adam's calling and responsibility was to protect the garden from the Devil because when the Devil gets in the garden, he will cause havoc. The Devil is sometimes the vehicle for the chaos we experience in our marriages, and in our lives. I know that we fuss and sometimes fight as couples and we think that it is the other person who is the problem. But that's exactly what the Devil wants. He wants you to believe that it's the other person who is the problem.

He wants you to believe that falsehood because he knows that you will never fix the real problem when the person you are fighting is not the real problem. The problem is a spiritual one brought on by our own sinful natures or by a rebellious and clever Enemy of God.

Until we recognize the covenantal aspect of transcendence in our marriages—that God instituted marriage and is therefore in charge, meaning that His viewpoint must be our viewpoint—we will never experience the productive, purposeful, and peaceful relationship we were designed to have. We will not experience it because we will continue to look at life through the limitations of physical eyes. We will miss out on the connections made in the spiritual realm.

Marriage is a covenantal agreement created to improve the ability of each partner to carry out on earth what God has designated in heaven.

A SUITABLE HELPER

Before God gave man a wife, He gave him a calling. He gave him a garden. He gave him a place to plant and protect. And He gave him a responsibility. But then He gave him something more.

We read in our passage as it continues,

Out of the ground the Lord God formed every beast of the field and every bird of the sky, and brought them to the man to see what he would call them; and whatever the man called a living creature, that was its name. The man gave names to all the cattle, and to the birds of the sky, and to every beast of the field, but for Adam there was not found a helper suitable for him. So the Lord God caused a deep sleep to fall upon the man, and he slept; then He took one of his ribs and closed up the flesh at that place. The Lord God fashioned into a woman the rib which He had taken from the man, and brought her to the man. (Genesis 2:19–22)

It looks like God is playing cupid here, doesn't it? He is being a matchmaker. God says, "Adam—you are good, but you are not that good. You are great, but you are not that great. Adam, you need help."

In order for Adam to do what God has told him to do, he is going to need help in doing it. He will never reach his maximum potential because he is incomplete. But he didn't know that, and so God had him start doing something that would reveal to him a need.

As Adam began naming the animals in the garden, he was in a position to see that every animal had a partner. Every Mr. Antelope had a Mrs. Antelope. Every Mr. Buffalo had a Mrs. Buffalo. Every Mr. Penguin had a Mrs. Penguin. Within the process of fulfilling his responsibility, God revealed to Adam his need.

God let Adam see what he was missing. Everyone else had someone else like them. Adam did not. Notice, God did not give Adam a wife until He first created the realization of needing one. We attach more value to something or someone when we believe that they are needed. One of the most common complaints I hear in counseling sessions with married couples is that one of the partners does not feel needed. In a covenantal union, both partners are needed.

God saw Adam and said, "It is not good" for him to be alone. In fact, this is the first thing that God declares to be "not good." Up until then, God has been saying that things are good. All that He has created has been good. But with Adam out there doing his thing all by himself, God said, "This is not good. This man needs help."

The question on the floor is, Help to do what?

FASHIONED AS A HELPER

Could it be that Adam needed help to get his clothes washed? Probably not, since he didn't have any. Or maybe he needed someone to clean out his empty coconut shell that he used for drinking water? Maybe he needed someone to wake him up on time to get to work so that he could continue naming the animals? Or to make sure that he got his breakfast? But then again, if that is the kind of help Adam needed, then any maid could do that.

We read in the Bible that God didn't make just any maid, instead He "fashioned" a woman for Adam. He crafted Eve. The word "fashion" is not the same word used when we read about God creating man. When God created man, He reached down to the ground and pretty much just threw some dirt together and said, "There— Man."

> GOD SAYS, "ADAM—YOU ARE GOOD, BUT YOU ARE NOT THAT GOOD. YOU ARE GREAT, BUT YOU ARE NOT THAT GREAT. ADAM, YOU NEED HELP."

But when we read about God creating Eve, it says He "fashioned" her. To "fashion" something means to build it intricately. God took Adam's rib, and with it He carefully crafted a woman. God made a woman by forming her to be a uniquely distinct yet suitable completion to the man. So now if Adam wanted his rib back, he would be getting back a lot more than he ever had to begin with.

God gave Adam a suitable helper to his need to carry out the instruction God had previously given, and that is to rule. God didn't give Eve to Adam just so he could have some company. God gave Eve to Adam so that he could have someone to collaborate with in achieving the goal for which he had been created.

God didn't fashion Eve out of nothing, ladies, just so she could exist either. He fashioned Eve out of Adam's rib so that she could have someone with whom to collaborate in her divine purpose of dominion as well.

COMPLEMENTING, NOT CONFLICTING

In light of God's plan for wholeness in marriage, one of the most uninformed statements that a husband or wife can make is, "We are not compatible." Sometimes it's expressed, "We don't have anything in common," or, "We are as different as night and day." Of course you are—if both of you were the same, one of you would be unnecessary! The reason you need each other is because you are different. One likes coffee, the other likes tea. One goes to bed early, the other stays up late.

One of the sweetest blessings God has given me is a woman who has a personality totally different from mine. I'm an outgoing, exuberant, public personality while my wife is sedate and serene. We are different, and that is according to God's plan. Because our personalities are in contrast, when I'm too outgoing, her reserve pulls me back, and when she is too reserved, my enthusiasm pulls her forward.

Occasionally this causes friction, because I become a little irritated when she's too sedate, and she becomes a little ruffled when I'm too outgoing. But the issue is not our differences; we're supposed to be different. The issue is making those God-given differences work for us instead of against us.

Since sin entered the world, we have lost our understanding of how to make differences complement one another. If we would simply look for what God is trying to teach us through the mate He has given us, we would be growing rather than griping.

You may say, "I don't believe God gave me my mate." It's too late for that conclusion! God will teach you how to love and learn from the one you're with anyway. You and your mate don't have any problems as a result of differences that cannot be solved by applying God's guidelines for making them complementary rather than conflicting.

ACCEPTING GOD'S HELPER

Focusing back on the men for a moment, I believe our culture has often skewed the way women are viewed, and I want to address this. The reason why God gives a man a wife is not so he can have a cook, maid, or hobby partner, but because the man does not have everything he needs to rule well. The word "helper" can best be explained as someone who is able to collaborate in order to fulfill a purpose. If there was no help, Adam could only rule partially. He could not rule completely.

Let me be more forward—the first reason that God created Eve had nothing to do with sexuality or procreation. It had everything to do with dominion. Animals can procreate, but animals were not created to have dominion. The thing that makes Adam and Eve different from the animals is that they were uniquely given the responsibility, and design, to rule.

When a man rejects the healthy collaborative presence of a woman, he has eclipsed the rule of God in his life. Therefore, he has limited what God is free to do in him and through him in giving him spiritual authority because he has refused the divinely ordained help.

Men, if God provides the help, it is because you need the help. If you don't use the help, you don't get the help. Thus, you do not exercise your full dominion to rule in the sphere in which God has placed you.

The word "suitable," as we look at this further, means an "essential contributor." That is someone who is specifically designed to compliment and complete. In other words, a woman's point of view is not extra information. It is essential information. A woman's presence is not merely ornamental. It is vital in furthering the opportunity for dominion.

Whenever a married man makes a major decision without consulting his mate about it first to get her in-depth perspective, he will make the decision without the necessary components needed to decide well.

Men will often argue their decisions logically. Women will not only bring their logic into the equation, but because God has created them with more neural connectors in the brain, He will give them a sense, or an intuition, about things as well. And while the man has been given the freedom to make the final decision as the head of the home, that headship role ought to take into full consideration the total input of the help he needs from the helper God has provided.

Part of that headship role is in recognizing that there is a person near to him who understands him and who can give him a perspective that he did not otherwise have. Therefore, any man who does not utilize his mate for her mind, her skills, her intellect, her training, and her giftedness is a fool.

Now, that doesn't mean God doesn't throw in some fun in there along the way as well. Don't get me wrong. Marriage also offers companionship, sexual union, and procreation. But the primary purpose for marriage, that we discover in Genesis, is to fully supply all that is needed for mankind to carry out this charge called "dominion."

Marriage is a covenantal union designed to strengthen the capacity and ability for each partner to rule the sphere where God has placed them. Through the principle of transcendence, God has established the framework for this union: The freedom to rule within the boundaries that He has set up. Within that framework we find great liberty and great authority, and we will discover, as we utilize this liberty and authority, that our decisions really do matter.

2

HIERARCHY: THE ORDER OF MARRIAGE

Not too long ago, I took my car into the dealership for a checkup. I had taken it in for its routine oil change as well as other normal maintenance that needed to be done.

Shortly after I dropped it off, I received a phone call from the dealership telling me that there were some issues with my vehicle. One of the primary ones was the wearing of my tires. My tires were not wearing evenly, or at the appropriate rate of attrition.

The mechanic on the other end of the line said, "Tony, the reason why your tires are problematic is because your alignment is off. Your car is not properly aligned, and it's showing up in how your tires are being worn."

I asked him what we should do, and if we should replace the tires. But he said, "Even if we replace your tires,
if you do not fix the alignment problem, you will mess up
something brand new with a problem that has never been
addressed concerning the alignment."

In other words, the problem that I saw—the wearing
thin of my tires—was not the real problem. The tires did-
n't cause their own wear. The problem was caused by something else. The "something else" was that things were not
aligned properly. And because things were not aligned
properly, there was unnecessary wear and tear on that which
I was counting on to get me from point A to point B.

When we look around at our marriages and families
today, there is a lot of wear and tear. There is a lot of wear
and tear on women who are being abused, neglected, and
negatively affected. There is a lot of wear and tear on children who are being indulged and/or forgotten. There is a
lot of wear and tear on men who are being usurped and
disrespected.

Most of the negative issues facing our society at large
can be directly traced to the breakdown of the family. Because of the redefining and dismantling of the home,
death has replaced life, conflict has replaced harmony,
and pain has replaced peace.

How do we resolve the social crisis that we are facing
in so many people's lives and in our communities throughout our nation and the world? We resolve this deteriora-
tive crisis through accepting and honoring the terms of
the marital covenant.

In our previous chapter, we saw that marriage is a covenantal union designed by God to fortify the means by which both husband and wife are to exercise dominion within the unique sphere that they have been positioned.

We also saw that the first of three fundamental aspects of the marriage covenant is transcendence. Transcendence simply means that God is both the author and the authority of the covenant. He came up with the idea, orchestrated its inception, created the partners, united the two, and established the parameters.

SECOND COVENANT FACET: HIERARCHY

I now want to talk about the second key facet of a marriage covenant, and this has to do with the wear and tear I referred to earlier that was experienced by my tires. This is because the second aspect of the covenantal union involves the concept called *hierarchy*. A hierarchy, simply defined, is a chain of command. It is an order that functions within a particular alignment.

Like automobiles that need to be properly aligned, covenants only work when they function in God's ordained order. The same wear and tear that showed up on my tires when my car was out of alignment shows up in our marriages, families, and societies when couples ignore this vital component of the covenant.

How did Satan disrupt the first marriage? He did so by switching the order in the relationship. He didn't go to Adam to make a decision. He went to Eve, on purpose. He swapped the order of alignment.

God told Adam before Eve was even created that from every tree in the garden you may freely eat except for the tree of the knowledge of good and evil. After God gave that instruction to Adam, it was then Adam's job to transfer that information to Eve, which he did. But the Devil showed up later and wanted to talk to Eve. Eve ended up in an in-depth dialogue apart from Adam about the instructions from God.

We read this dialogue, and more, in chapter 3 of Genesis.

> Now the serpent was more crafty than any beast of the field which the Lord God had made. And he said to the woman, "Indeed, has God said, 'You shall not eat from any tree of the garden?'" The woman said to the serpent, "From the fruit of the trees of the garden we may eat; but from the fruit of the tree which is in the middle of the garden, God has said, 'You shall not eat from it or touch it, or you will die.'" The serpent said to the woman, "You surely will not die! For God knows that in the day you eat from it your eyes will be opened, and you will be like God, knowing good and evil." When the woman saw that the tree was good for food, and that it was a delight to the eyes, and that the tree was desirable to make one wise, she took from its fruit and ate; and she gave also to her husband with her, and he ate. (Genesis 3:1–6)

HOW DID SATAN DISRUPT THE FIRST MARRIAGE? HE DID SO BY SWITCHING THE ORDER IN THE RELATIONSHIP. HE DIDN'T GO TO ADAM TO MAKE A DECISION. HE WENT TO EVE, ON PURPOSE. HE SWAPPED THE ORDER OF ALIGNMENT.

Let's look at that last part again. It says that when Eve saw that the tree was "good for food, and that it was a delight to the eyes, and that the tree was desirable to make one wise," she partook of the fruit. Eve made a deliberate decision based on an emotional response. The tree both "delighted" her and caused her to "desire" it. What happens next is that she then gave the fruit to Adam.

Where was Adam all along? He was "with her." It wasn't that Adam wasn't around and Eve just got played by a fast-rapping snake; Adam was right there with her. Eve had become the spiritual leader between the two. Adam had become a passive responder. The roles got reversed, and all hell broke loose.

Whenever the man gives up his spiritual headship, and whenever a woman takes over that spiritual headship, that is an invitation to the Devil to come into the garden. Satan is invited when roles get flipped. Today we have a generation of flipped roles, dominant women and passive men who are not following the biblical mandate of alignment.

What would have happened to my car if I would have told the mechanic not to worry about the warning of the wear and tear on my tires and to just leave the car out of alignment? I would have kept driving my car and eventually the thing would have become shaky. It would have become too shaky to drive properly. Not only does a vehicle wear out its tires when it is out of alignment, it also stops providing a stable environment for its passengers. A shaky vehicle is a danger to others who are on the road as well. Everyone suffers.

Many marriages are shaky today because the relationship is out of alignment. Just like Adam who said nothing while listening to the snake smooth-talk his wife into making a monumental decision, men, and women, are reversing the order in which things are to be run in the home today.

Nature abhors a vacuum. When a man shrinks from his role of headship, it is to be expected that a woman will step in to fill it.

BIBLICAL ALIGNMENT

Where do we find this biblical outline of alignment? We find it when we look at what Paul writes in the book of

1 Corinthians. Please notice that he is writing to Christians at the church in Corinth, addressing a group of believers. We read, "But I want you to understand that Christ is the head of every man, and the man is the head of a woman, and God is the head of Christ" (1 Corinthians 11:3).

Paul says that he wants us to understand that there is an order to how God operates. That order clearly designates that God is the head of Christ. It also states that Christ is the head of every man. And that the man is the head of *a* woman—not *all* women, I want to point out, but *a* woman. This alignment does not state that all men are over all women, nor that this arrangement applies in a work environment or other relationships. This is clearly talking about alignment in marriage because it says "*a* woman."

This passage is where we get the clearest delineation of God's functional alignment. God, the Father, is over Christ. Christ is over all men. And a man (husband) is over a woman (wife).

When anyone gets out of that order, Satan has an opportunity to manifest chaos. Keep in mind that we discover from that passage that even Jesus cannot get out of alignment. If Jesus can't get out of this hierarchy, then you and I certainly cannot either.

Jesus Christ is God in the flesh. Jesus Christ is the Son of the living God who bears the very essence of Deity. Yet when it comes to function within history, He is under authority. When it comes to how Christ operates within the realm of space and time, He is beneath prescribed authority.

When speaking about Himself to His disciples while in Samaria, Jesus said that He had come "to do the will of Him who sent Me and to accomplish His work" (John 4:34). In other words, He was underneath Another's authority.

Christ's ontological being is the same essence as God, as we read in the first chapter of Hebrews, but when it came to functioning on earth, Jesus placed Himself underneath God to carry out His divine plan.

The work of redemption got completed because Jesus came under the headship of the Father. Redemption, sanctification, glorification, and eternal life were accomplished through a system of hierarchy. Jesus operated under authority in order to carry out the kingdom agenda on earth.

CHRIST AS THE HEAD

We also read in 1 Corinthians 11:3 that every man is underneath Christ. It is at this stage, let me point out, where we often find our breakdown in the chain of command. We don't have a breakdown with Jesus being underneath God, the Father. Jesus was perfectly obedient to the Father. He said, "Not My will, but Yours be done" (Luke 22:42). Jesus demonstrated this submission even to the extent of death, and death on a cross.

The breakdown in hierarchy typically comes on level number two. This is where every man is supposed to be under the authority of Jesus Christ. In fact, this hierarchy supplies us with the biblical definition of a man. The biblical definition of a man is a male who has learned to operate under the lordship of Jesus Christ over his life.

What many men complain about concerning their wives not submitting to them is often also true about them. Men often say that their wives will not submit. But the question we get in response through Paul's words in 1 Corinthians is, "Are you submitting?" Because if the man is not submitting to his rightful authority, then what he is seeing in his wife is simply a reflection of his own disorder.

I know that "submission" is an unpopular word. But when we understand submission from a biblical perspective, we will see that it is a positive force to accomplish good, not a negative force to subject someone to an inferior status. The Greek word for submission, *hupotasso*, means to place oneself under the authority of another.

This does not involve coercion but rather a willingness to take who and what God made you and submit it to the authority of another: in a man's case, to God; in a woman's case, to God and to her husband.

It is the lack of submission by a man that generally leads to the lack of submission by a woman. What men often want to do is to be a "head" without being underneath their "Head." The problems in a marriage come when men are out of alignment, and then try to get their wives to get into alignment under them. Next, the kids get out of alignment as well, and pretty soon the entire family is in chaos.

It starts with Christ, then moves to the man. We discover more about this in Exodus chapter 34, when God says something very interesting about men. We read,

Three times a year all your males are to appear before
the Lord God, the God of Israel. For I will drive out
nations before you and enlarge your borders, and no
man shall covet your land when you go up three times
a year to appear before the Lord your God. (Exodus
34:23–24)

> ## IT IS THE LACK OF SUBMISSION BY A MAN THAT GENERALLY LEADS TO THE LACK OF SUBMISSION BY A WOMAN. WHAT MEN OFTEN WANT TO DO IS TO BE A "HEAD" WITHOUT BEING UNDERNEATH THEIR "HEAD."

Three times a year all the males in Israel were to go on
a retreat before the Lord who ruled over them. In the Old
Testament, the phrase "Lord your God" means "sovereign
Lord." A sovereign is someone who is in authority over
you, and who tells you what to do. We talked about the
sovereign aspect of God in a covenant when we looked at
transcendence earlier.

Three times a year, as we see from this passage, all

men were to go to a certain location, and in so doing, acknowledge the sovereign rule of God in their lives. Now, before we move past that too quickly, let's look at what that might have done to those left behind.

Three times a year all of the males left their land and homes. From a military and defense perspective, that is unthinkable. From a commerce and agricultural perspective, that is unthinkable. All the men are gone and there are only women and children left to fend for themselves? That doesn't sound like a very good national strategy.

But that is where the second verse in that passage comes in. God says that while you are away seeking Me and honoring Me under My authority, men, do not worry. He says that He will see to it that no one will bother your land, houses, or anyone left behind. We read, "no man shall covet your land when you go up . . . to appear before the Lord your God."

In other words, God is saying that if you will simply align yourself underneath My authority, then I've got your back. I have you covered. I've got it. But in order for God to cover us, men, we are going to have to humble ourselves underneath His authority. We are going to have to align our thoughts, our actions, our decisions, our leadership underneath the overarching viewpoint and authority of God.

What Satan wants men to do is to claim headship without being underneath Headship. And you can always know when Satan has been successful in carrying out this scheme. You can tell when a man is not underneath divine Headship because he rarely, if ever, brings God's point of view into the discussion. His decisions, or the decisions of the family, do not reflect God's decisions. Yet, as a reminder, whoever is ultimately making the decisions, it will be the man who is held responsible.

Remember that it was Eve who talked to the Devil in the garden and chose to eat the fruit. But it is Adam who is blamed for sin entering the world. We read in the New Testament that "in Adam all die" (1 Corinthians 15:22a). Why Adam? Because he was responsible. To be the head over someone means that you are responsible.

Because we are held responsible, men, we need to keep in mind that Christ is the One who is perfect, and not us. We need to be under Him. We don't know enough to lead correctly. So what we must do as men is to find out what the sovereign Lord's will is for every area of our lives. We need to go before the Lord our God, and then lead our family in that direction. When we do that, God says He will protect, guide, and inform us.

The best thing that a man can do in leading his home and cultivating his marriage is to raise the question, "What is the mind of Christ on this matter?" and then follow it. Once you have done that, you will have your wife's full attention, and submission. Because now she is no longer arguing with you and your opinions. Now you have brought Christ and His word into the equation. Eventually she will relax when she sees that you are underneath an authority that can be trusted.

One of women's greatest needs in marriage is for security. A woman needs to feel secure, and that is why a woman will sometimes ask her husband to hold her. Most men misinterpret that as a request for physical intimacy, but if the emotional need for security is on her mind, she is not thinking about physical desires.

A wife needs to feel secure. A man must align himself under the Word of God to offer an environment that causes her to feel that way. When he does that, he will be demonstrating what it means to be a truly spiritual leader over her.

Marriage is a covenantal union put in place to demonstrate God's sovereignty within the hierarchy of our dominion. Christ is under God, the Father. All men are under Christ. And the man is over a woman.

EQUAL VALUE, DIFFERENT FUNCTIONS

Now, keep in mind that hierarchy does not determine value. We, men and women, are all equal under God. Hierarchy is a key aspect of a covenant that defines function. A man is functionally subordinate under Christ, but not of higher value than a woman. A woman is functionally subordinate under a man, but not of lesser value.

The Bible gives us a reason for this positioning and we read it in 1 Timothy, chapter 2. It says,

But I do not allow a woman to teach or exercise authority over a man, but to remain quiet. For it was Adam who was first created, and then Eve. And it was not Adam who was deceived, but the woman being deceived, fell into transgression. (1 Timothy 2:12–14)

Please notice that Paul presents this principle based on the order of the church. This has nothing to do with the local culture, or the time period. This has nothing to do with how a person was raised. Paul says that this one goes all the way back to when there was no sin in the world. He says that God created Adam first. So there was an order. And then came Eve.

Then he says that it was not Adam who was deceived, but that it was Eve. Through this passage, we are seeing the clear order of creation, and how that order got reversed.

When Eve ate from the Tree of the Knowledge of Good and Evil, and then persuaded Adam to do the same, what was being revealed was a desire to live life independently of God. That is the way most relationships function today. One or both partners choose to live their lives separately from God's rule and authority.

Conflicts also arise because you and your spouse have different histories, learning styles, personalities, and backgrounds. One spouse might say, "My father raised me like this," or "My mother always did that." Everyone tends to operate from a different viewpoint because they have their own idea of what makes up the knowledge of good and evil—what is right and what is wrong.

Everyone has an opinion. The problem is that you can spend the rest of your lives arguing over opinions. Scripture says that is not the way to live life. We are to live life based on revelation, and not personal inclination. Whatever issue is causing friction in our marriage, or whatever decision needs to be made—whether it be financial, personal, or professional—what we must do is discover God's viewpoint on the matter and align ourselves under Him.

Adam was to make it his priority to hear God's viewpoint on issues pertaining to life and the family, and then disseminate that to the other members of the family through discipleship and leadership. If couples will ever decide for men to lead first according to God's principles, and that women will reflect their leadership underneath them, it will change everything in your home.

> WHEN EVE ATE FROM THE TREE OF THE KNOWLEDGE OF GOOD AND EVIL, AND THEN PERSUADED ADAM TO DO THE SAME, WHAT WAS BEING REVEALED WAS A DESIRE TO LIVE LIFE INDEPENDENTLY OF GOD.

Now, let me just briefly state that this order does have its limitations. If a man asks his wife to rob a bank, should she rob the bank? No, she should not rob the bank because that is breaking a greater law. That would be breaking

God's law not to steal. In other words, if a man asks his wife to do anything that is contrary to God's laws, then he yields his authority over her to God.

A husband does not have absolute authority over his wife. His authority remains valid as long as he's not violating a divine mandate, Scripture, or principle from the Word of God.

IT IS TIME TO ALIGN

So far we have seen that God has created us for the divinely appointed purpose of exercising dominion over the sphere of our world where we have responsibility and influence. We are to rule in that sphere in concert with God and underneath Him as His subordinate in a prescribed chain of command.

God first created Adam and gave him fulfillment in his calling of rulership. As Adam carried out that calling, God supplied Adam with a woman who was uniquely fashioned to become a suitable helper in this mandate of dominion.

We noted earlier that a helpmate is more than someone who cooks, cleans, and wipes noses. A helper is someone who is enabled to use her gifts, skills, and insights to partner with her husband in such a way as to make the union more complete and adequate for dominion.

We also highlighted that it was God who initiated and created the first marital union, providing Him with the ultimate authority through transcendence on how the partnership should be run. God performed the first wedding ceremony, joining Adam and Eve together as "one flesh" (Genesis 2:24).

Then, we learned that within the marriage covenant, God has an established hierarchy—or chain of command. Christ is under God, the Father. All men are under Christ. A woman is under a man.

Based on these truths, here is what needs to be decided. First, the men need to decide to come underneath spiritual authority. And I'm not talking about some ethereal, amorphous spiritual authority. Jesus Christ has expressed His authority on earth through His word and the church, so that means men must come underneath God and the church in order to study, learn, apply, and abide by His words and truth. Men must then become the pastors of their own homes underneath God's authority, and they must represent Christ and His leadership within the home through ongoing discipleship, relationship-building, and decision-making.

Then, ladies, you will need to reflect that leadership through submitting to your husband as leader, and encouraging him in his leadership within the home. You will need to yield to his direction, pray for his growth and ability to lead you and your family well, and ultimately trust that God will cover you when you are properly aligned underneath His prescribed hierarchy.

CLIMATE CONTROL

However, I tend to put a greater emphasis on the role of a man when I talk about marriage. I do this for two reasons. One, because men are the head of the home and therefore held responsible. And two, because men often have the ability to control the climate in their homes.

When God made woman, He made her to be a receiver and responder. He made her a little softer, a little warmer, a little more emotional in order to respond to man. In other words, a woman responds to a man in such a way that the very thing the husband wants, he will receive by giving, not by demanding.

God does not want a wife to love her husband and respond to him because he demands it; God wants her to do it as a natural response. God wants a wife to respond because a husband meets her emotional needs with loving care, because he wears her out with love and attention.

I tell many men who come to me for marital counseling, "Stop pushing so hard and start loving a little more. Stop complaining so much, and start loving a little harder." If a husband lets his wife know she is loved and makes her feel secure, he won't have to worry about her fulfilling her responsibility to the home. He won't have to wonder if he will have an active, frequent physical relationship. She will be right there responding to his needs.

But one must lead in the sense God intended. You must say, "Guys, I can't hang out with you tonight. I've got a wife at home I want to spend time with. I think I'll take her out tonight." I will guarantee you that when you are that kind of husband, you will get the kind of response you want without demanding it.

Some of you men may be saying, "Tony, I'm trying.

How come my wife isn't responding?" Let me answer that with an illustration. A man can become angry with his wife at 10:00 p.m. and be over it by 10:30 p.m. "Come on, honey," he will say, "we need to spend some time together." He previously was a powder keg with a short fuse, but in thirty minutes his whole demeanor has changed.

On the other hand, if a wife becomes angry with her husband at ten in the morning, she may still be angry at ten o'clock that night—and sometimes the night after that.

The reason a wife stays mad is because her emotions have been rubbed the wrong way. But a husband can smooth them by stroking them the right way. A husband can bring her back if he takes the time to learn how. It takes what is called *unconditional love*—that is, love based on a decision to love no matter how difficult the way, with or without response.

For many husbands, loving unconditionally is going to require an apology and a new start. "I've failed. I haven't loved you the way I was supposed to love you, and I know that it has affected our relationship. I'm going to change. I'm going to love you deeply the way you need to be loved."

It's going to take that kind of commitment to succeed in marriage. For some men that will be a new decision, while for others it will be a continuation of a commitment already made. New or old, it will be worth it.

Psalm 128 contains an interesting note on the response nature of women and how that affects the home.

It says that a man who fears the Lord (a man who walks with God) will find his wife becoming like a fruitful grapevine in his house. In a favorable climate grapevines need no coaxing to grow. Given the right environment, they will grow and produce grapes from which wine, a drink symbolizing celebration and happiness in biblical times, is made. It is the same in the home.

The husband is responsible for creating a climate in which his wife can flourish. When that happens, he can naturally expect a joyful response. The husband can anticipate joy from his labor.

Climate control involves a number of requirements. First, the husband must be at home enough to create and maintain an ideal temperature. The husband who is rarely at home cannot do that because his absences frustrate his wife and damage her self-confidence. Second, the husband must know what his wife needs in order for her to grow. That means he must spend quality time with his mate if he is going to receive a quality response.

The west wall of a house in which I once lived was covered with a vine. Each summer that vine grew very quickly. Summer rains and the warmth of the sun encouraged it to cover the wall with gorgeous foliage. In no time at all it had to be trimmed and then trimmed again as it began to grow under the window trim, through the brick exterior, and under the roof of the house. This vine brought me great enjoyment because of its growth.

So it is with a wife who finds her husband providing the right climate. She will bring great enjoyment to him with her love, providing him with the atmosphere he needs and desires. The better and more constant the climate, the better, faster, and more consistent the wife's growth will be. As she grows and is fulfilled, her husband will benefit from her growth.

> THE HUSBAND IS RESPONSIBLE FOR CREATING A CLIMATE IN WHICH HIS WIFE CAN FLOURISH. WHEN THAT HAPPENS, HE CAN NATURALLY EXPECT A JOYFUL RESPONSE. THE HUSBAND CAN ANTICIPATE JOY FROM HIS LABOR.

The marital union is a covenant created for the express purpose of uniting two beings into one. This is done in an effort to equip both partners with the tools necessary to exercise dominion in their lives. Understanding the nature of a covenant, transcendence, and hierarchy—as well as the third element we will look at in the next chapter—makes it possible to abide by the terms of the covenant, enabling us to receive the benefits we so greatly want to enjoy.

3

ETHICS:
THE OPERATION
OF MARRIAGE

When my son Anthony was younger, I bought him a bike for Christmas. The bike came disassembled with a thick set of instructions. Now, I assumed that I was an intelligent man. I was working on my seminary degree at the time at one of the most prestigious theological institutions in the nation. I didn't think that I needed to read a set of rules on how to put a simple bike together for my son.

So I set in motion the process of putting the bike together on my own. Eight hours later, with just the handlebars assembled, my wife gave me a suggestion. She said, "Tony, why don't you read the instructions?"

What Lois was saying, even though she didn't say it

in these exact words, was that the bicycle maker certainly must know more about how to assemble a bike than I did.

Lois was right. I swallowed my pride, read the instructions, and assembled the bike in just forty-five minutes. What I hadn't been able to do on my own in eight hours was accomplished in less than one simply because the bicycle maker knew more about bikes than I did. The manufacturer had created and designed the bike to begin with, so it only made sense that they would know the rules to follow in putting it together.

THIRD COVENANT FACET: ETHICS

We've seen in our previous chapters that God is both the creator and designer of the marriage covenant. He is transcendent over the union. He has also set in place a hierarchy—a chain of command—for functionality within the relationship. In this chapter, we are going to look at the final aspect of a covenant: ethics.

I go into greater detail on the subject of this chapter in the companion guides to this one titled *For Married Men Only* and *For Married Women Only*. While we will touch on the basics of this facet of a covenant in this chapter, I want to encourage you to get and read the other two marriage guides. There is too much vital information on this topic to include in the limited space remaining. But for the purpose of understanding and applying the power of a marital covenant in our lives, what I cover now will provide all that we need in order to do that.

Ethics involves three interdependent elements: rules, sanctions, and continuity.

AUTHORITY AND THE COVENANT

If you were to come over to my house, I would welcome you inside but there would be a set of rules by which to abide. Just like I would need to abide by the rules for your house. For example, in my home, I don't allow smoking. So if you smoke, you would need to put out your cigarette before you came in my home.

I am able to make these rules and enforce them because it is my house. Marriage is God's house. He came up with the idea. And it can only run right when it is run by His rules.

In a covenant, there are always rules. However, please note, you don't get to make the rules—that is, unless you are the authority over the covenant. Since God is transcendent, He is the authority over the marriage covenant. Therefore, God has established the rules for a successful marriage.

What married couples often want to do, though, is to have God's institution of marriage, yet run it by their own rules. They want to get married in the church so that God will bless their marriage, but then they want to leave God standing at the altar. They want to make up their own rules for how a marriage should be run.

Let me tell you a secret. It is a very powerful secret. Pay attention: You don't get God's results without operating by God's rules. You don't get God's blessings in your marriage, and in your home, without following God's instructions. You don't enjoy God's provision, protection, and peace in your relationships without abiding by God's policies concerning the covenantal union of marriage.

You can spend eight hours arguing with your spouse and still never resolve the issue when, if you had followed God's rules, the discussion could have been over in a matter of minutes. And both parties could have been satisfied at the end of the process. What we so often try to do is come up with our own rules, and then wonder why it is taking so long to get things right.

As I said earlier, all covenants have rules. But the authority establishes those rules over the covenant, and no one else. In the case of a marriage covenant, that authority is God.

TWO RULES FOR MARRIAGE

God clearly illustrated the use of covenantal rules when He instituted the Mosaic covenant. In the Mosaic covenant, God told the Israelites to do certain things, and not to do certain other things. He listed these rules in the Ten Commandments.

In the marriage covenant, we also find His set of rules. There aren't ten of them and they aren't carved in stone, but they are just as clearly understandable as the ones given to Moses. In marriage, there are only two rules. God has made it really easy for us. If a couple will simply abide by these two rules, everything in their home will change.

We find these two rules in the book of Ephesians, chapter 5. God boils down the two rules for an enjoyable and functioning marriage into just one verse. We read,

"Nevertheless, each individual among you also is to love his own wife even as himself, and the wife must see to it that she respects her husband" (Ephesians 5:33).

Love and respect. The beginning foundation of what there is to say about the ethics of a marriage can be narrowed down to two simple words: love and respect.

Love as Christ Loved

First, God says that husbands are to love their wives. This is not only a command, it is also a critical piece of the covenant.

We often throw the word "love" around loosely, leaving it to be defined in many ways. People say things like, "I love chocolate cake," "I love football," or "I love that show." The words they really mean when they say that are "like" or "enjoy." The definition of love goes much deeper than what we feel emotionally attached to. As I mentioned earlier, to "love" is to passionately and righteously pursue the well-being of another.

The Bible says in 1 John 4:8 that "God is love." Since God *is* love, love must always be defined with God as the standard.

Love involves emotions, sure, but it also includes a conscious pursuit of good for the other person involved. Love's first concern is, How does this action contribute to the recipient of my love's well-being? If it doesn't, or if it does the opposite, then it is not love.

Husbands should not get their cues on how to love their wives from the television, their friends, or the culture.

Men, we are to get our example on how to love from God. Christ is our standard.

> # THE BEGINNING FOUNDATION OF WHAT THERE IS TO SAY ABOUT THE ETHICS OF A MARRIAGE CAN BE NARROWED DOWN TO TWO SIMPLE WORDS: LOVE AND RESPECT.

Let's go back a few verses in the book of Ephesians that we looked at earlier and read it closely. It states,

Husbands, love your wives, just as Christ also loved the church and gave Himself up for her, so that He might sanctify her, having cleansed her by the washing of water with the word, that He might present to Himself the church in all her glory, having no spot or wrinkle or any such thing; but that she would be holy and blameless. So husbands ought also to love their own wives as their own bodies. He who loves his own wife loves himself; for no one ever hated his own flesh, but nourishes and cherishes it, just as Christ also does the church, because we are members of His body. For this reason a man shall leave his father and mother and shall be joined to his wife, and the two shall become one flesh. (Ephesians 5:25–31)

As we saw in the previous chapter, from the standpoint of hierarchy, men are aligned underneath Christ. Men are to love their wives just as Christ has done in His example of loving the church. The question is, How did Christ love the church?

There are three ways that we see how Christ loved the church from this passage. Christ became the church's savior, sanctifier, and satisfier.

Savior

The first way Christ loved the church was by being the church's savior. We read that He "gave Himself up for her."

Saving involves sacrificing. Christ sacrificed for the church, and men ought to sacrifice for the benefit of their wives. Your wife will know that you love her, men, when you are willing to give up things that are important to you for something that your wife legitimately needs for her well-being. It may cost you something. It may cost you time, energy, money, or a delayed, or reduced, achievement of a goal that you have, but that is because it is a sacrifice.

When King David went to make a sacrifice before God to petition Him to hold back a plague put on his people, he purchased the land on which he was making the sacrifice. He bought it even though it had been offered to him for free.

Why did he purchase it? Because he said, "I insist on paying you for it. I will not sacrifice to the Lord my God burnt offerings that cost me nothing" (2 Samuel 24:24 NIV). David knew that the nature of a sacrifice meant that you had to give up something in the process. Men, what are you giving up in order to love your wives?

A man confided in me once, "Tony, my wife is killing me."

I replied, "You told me that you wanted to be like Jesus, didn't you?" Jesus became our Savior because of love, even though it killed Him in the process.

Remember, Adam also had to sacrifice something, a rib, in order to get Eve. He had to give up something too. We have men today who want to be married, but they still want to function as a single. They don't want to sacrifice any strategic time, strategic attention, or resources for the benefit of their wives. These men don't want a wife; they want a maid. They want to marry someone just so they can be served.

The covenantal union of marriage was instituted so that men and women would work together in carrying out their mandate of dominion. But there will be no dominion in your home, workplace, or world if you will not abide by the rules of the covenant. Men are commanded to love. Love involves sacrifice.

Sanctifier

The second way Christ loved the church was "so that He might sanctify her." Christ not only became the church's Savior, He became the church's Sanctifier. "Sanctify" is a theological term meaning "to take something from where it is, and turn it into what it ought to be." Sanctification is the process of spiritual transformation.

A husband is to be his wife's sanctifier. He is to act as a transforming agent in her life, for good. When a man marries a woman, he not only marries a woman, but he also marries her history. He marries everything that made her the way she is—all of those things that she cleverly hid from him while they were dating.

After he marries her, he may say, "I didn't know she screamed." Well, she has always screamed. She just never let you see it because she wasn't going to do anything to jeopardize that ring. She camouflaged it. Of course, the guys do the same thing.

> **A HUSBAND IS TO BE HIS WIFE'S SANCTIFIER. HE IS TO ACT AS A TRANSFORMING AGENT IN HER LIFE, FOR GOOD.**

Becoming your wife's sanctifier means becoming a tool in the hand of God to bring about a positive transformation in your wife. How is this done? We read that Christ did it by "the washing of water with the word."

Christ did it through living and teaching Truth. He did it not only by discipling, but also by modeling a life fully aligned with the principles in God's Word.

Satisfier

The third way Christ loved the church was by becoming its Satisfier. The Bible passage we looked at earlier said, "He who loves his own wife loves himself; for no one ever hated his own flesh, but nourishes and cherishes it, just as Christ also does the church, because we are members of His body."

Men ought to become their wives' satisfier. You do this by valuing your wife in the same degree that you value yourself. Whatever you would do for your own well-being, you ought to be willing to do for her.

The wife must be viewed as what 1 Peter 3:7 calls a "fellow heir"—an equal partner. Her opinion matters. Her authority matters. Her thoughts matter. Her perspective matters. Her presence matters. Yes, men, you are the head, and you get to make the final decision, but her viewpoint must be fully heard, and fully valued, before you make that decision.

If you will become your wife's satisfier, she will respond to you the way you want her to. She will respond because she will feel cherished and valued.

You say, "But Tony, my wife has become hardened and calloused. She is as cold as ice." My answer is simple: Warm her up, and watch her melt. Ice only stays ice in a cold environment. What we often do is complain about our wife without being willing to change the environment in an effort to evoke a change in her.

It starts with the men. The man is the thermostat in the marriage. The wife is the thermometer. Don't expect a summer wife if you bring home winter weather. A wife must experience love. She must know that her husband is her savior, sanctifier, and satisfier in a covenantal commitment to her, just like Christ is to the church.

Respect Your Man

While it may start with the man, ladies, you need to realize that a bad wife can ruin a good husband. So what makes a woman a bad wife? A bad wife is a woman who does not respect her husband. We read about this second rule in the covenantal union of marriage in Ephesians, as we saw earlier, where it said,

> Nevertheless, each individual among you also is to love his own wife even as himself, and the wife must see to it that she respects her husband. (Ephesians 5:33)

The first thing I want us to see from this passage is a little word with a lot of meaning. The word is "must." This word "must" means that this is a command. The command for a woman to respect her husband is not an option. It is a rule of the covenant.

What is interesting here is that it doesn't say that women must "love" their husbands—although the overarching rule of love given in the Scripture that we "love one another"

(1 John 4:7) applies. What a woman is commanded to do, as a rule of the marriage covenant, is to *respect* her husband.

Ladies, your husband doesn't need you to love him as much as he needs you to respect him. To respect your husband is to hold him in high esteem and honor. What a woman needs from a man is located in her heart. What a man needs from a woman is located in his head. It is called his ego.

Women will often say to a man, "I'm not going to feed your ego." But that is sort of like him saying to her, "I am not going to feed your heart." Men long to have their egos fed. They want their egos fed so badly that they will often feed it themselves, even if it means lying to feed it. You know what I'm talking about, men. Tell the truth, and shame the Devil. We do.

A wife is able to feed a man's ego in a legitimate manner when she respects and honors him. There is nothing more dangerous to a marriage relationship than disrespect. When a man does not feel like he is respected, he will either rebel against the woman, remove himself from her, or become passive.

It reminds me of the story of Winston Churchill and Lady Astor in the British Parliament. These two individuals despised each other. One day, Lady Astor said to Winston Churchill, "Winston, if you were my husband, I would put poison in your tea."

Winston replied, "Lady Astor, if you were my wife, I would drink it."

But, seriously, when the rules of a relational covenant

are broken, all parties suffer. A wife "must see to it that she respects her husband." This is a rule of the covenant.

> LADIES, YOUR HUSBAND DOESN'T NEED YOU TO LOVE HIM AS MUCH AS HE NEEDS YOU TO RESPECT HIM. TO RESPECT YOUR HUSBAND IS TO HOLD HIM IN HIGH ESTEEM AND HONOR.

In the Old Testament covenants, as we will see shortly, obedience to the terms of the covenant brought blessing. And disobedience to the terms of the covenant brought chaos. Wives, to show respect to your husband is not an option. It is a command.

If a policeman pulls you over and you think he was wrong, you will not jump, scream, and call him names all the while telling him that he is a fool. You will get yourself locked up if you do something like that, because even if the policeman is wrong, he still holds a position of authority, and expects your respect.

Many wives are out of order in the marriage union because of the way that they are behaving. Whether your husband has earned—or in your mind deserves—your respect is beside the point. God has commanded wives to respect their husbands by virtue of their position.

There are only two rules in a marital covenant. But those two rules can either produce life or bring about an early death—death in harmony, purpose, and productivity, and especially death in the areas of dominion, blessing, and continuity (more on this in a moment).

God is looking at how the fundamentals of a covenant are being honored in your marriage in order to respond to you accordingly. He is looking at the husband to see how he displays his love for his wife through his actions. He is looking at the wife to see how she respects her husband.

He is looking because He is going to respond to you based on your actions to deliver what we are going to look at in the remainder of this chapter—either blessings or curses. So many of us are blocking our blessings today because we are defying God's order. So many of us are living broken, tired lives today because we are defaulting on the terms of the covenant.

God has enabled each of us to enjoy His abundance on earth, but it must be done within the structure of a covenant. God is transcendent, and in His transcendence, He has given us a code of ethics that must be followed. If we do, we will experience benefits. If we don't, we will experience the loss that comes as a result.

SANCTIONS

These benefits and losses that are found within the aspect of ethics in a covenant are very important. In fact, they are dangerously important. It is essential that they be understood because when they are not understood there is little dominion and enjoyment from the marriage, and much pain. I want to be intentionally didactic in covering this next section because my goal right now is to offer you pristine clarity on an often misunderstood reality.

We call these benefits and losses *sanctions*. It is the term used to describe the blessings and the curses that accompany the covenant. All covenants have blessings and curses attached to them. One contemporary way we often phrase it, without realizing that we are describing an aspect of sanctions, is by using the terminology "cause and effect."

Cause and effect, of which the effect is blessings and curses, simply means that attached to the covenant are certain effects set in place to occur when the other aspects of the covenant are either adhered to or not adhered to.

God told Moses, as we read in chapters 28 and 29 of the book of Deuteronomy, the various blessings and curses that would fall on the Israelites if they either obeyed or did not obey Him. He said, in essence, that if they followed His covenant, they could expect to receive all of these different blessings. It wasn't that they *might* receive them, He promised them.

Conversely, God was saying, if they did not follow the terms of His covenant, then they could expect to receive the different curses that He outlined as well. God gave the cause: obedience or disobedience. Then He gave the effect: blessing or curse. It was up to them to choose, once again reinforcing our mandate to exercise dominion in our lives.

After detailing the many blessings and curses to the Israelites, God said something else that is an important thing to note for our study together on the marriage covenant. In verse 9 of chapter 29, we read, "So keep the words of this covenant to do them, that you may prosper in all that you do."

In other words, God is saying to them that He is making this covenant for them so that they can benefit. When a man is interested in making a marriage covenant with a woman, he will often make promises attached to the covenant. He will tell her all of the ways that she is going to benefit by aligning herself with him. What he is doing is letting her know the benefits, or blessings, that will accrue by entering into that relationship.

In the verse we just looked at, God is letting them know that if they will simply adhere to their part of the covenant, He promises to carry out the things that He said He would do in response. Marriage has been designed as a tool by God to bring about good in your life. Unfortunately, because we so often do not understand the true nature and purpose of marriage, we lose sight of that truth and end up living lives characterized by chaos.

A lot of the stuff that we fight about as couples has nothing to do with the stuff that we are fighting about. It has to do with the curses, and demonic realm working within those curses. One little thing can easily turn into an argument that puts a couple on the path to the divorce court. And you end up wondering how one little thing could do that.

It can do that because it's not the one little thing. It is the breaking of the marriage covenant either through a lack of submission under the transcendence of God, a lack of alignment, or a breaking of the covenantal rules of love and respect within the code of ethics.

It's like asking how one small piece of fruit in the garden of Eden could have caused so much pain? It caused so much pain for all generations to come because it wasn't just about a piece of fruit. It was about the effect: the curse, which came from the cause— disobedience to God's rule.

Couples, if we cannot grasp the seriousness of making a spiritual connection in everything that goes on in our marriages, we will continue to rant and rave about the fruit, or whatever the current issue is. We will continue to focus on the thing that is happening without realizing that we must align ourselves under the fundamentals of a covenant in order to be in a position to receive the blessings that God has promised.

Family counseling that gives advice on relational techniques is good and I recommend it when marriages have reached an impasse in communication. But in order to reverse the effects of curses in your home and lives, and in order to evoke a blessing in your sphere of dominion, you will need more than that. You will need to address the spiritual issue, and a spiritual issue can only be addressed spiritually.

If you want to get back on the blessing side of things and away from the cursing side of things in your home, you must change the way you function in accordance with the covenant. Understanding and owning the truth concerning sanctions can save more than your marriage; it can save your life.

OATHS AND SEXUAL INTIMACY

In the Bible, sanctions are often attached to oaths. An oath is a spiritually binding declaration. When a couple gets married, they make a spiritually and legally binding oath to each other. This legally binding oath includes sanctions that can involve the level at which God actively participates in their lives, as well as other sanctions reaching down into the lives of their children. We read about this in Malachi chapter 2 where it says,

> This is another thing you do: you cover the altar of the Lord with tears, with weeping and with groaning, because He no longer regards the offering or accepts it with favor from your hand. Yet you say, "For what reason?" Because the Lord has been a witness between you and the wife of your youth, against whom you have dealt treacherously, though she is your companion and your wife by covenant. But not one has done so who has a remnant of the Spirit. And what did that one do while he was seeking a godly offspring? Take heed then to your spirit, and let no one deal treacherously against the wife of your youth. (Malachi 2:13–15)

In this passage, we see that God has positioned Himself to no longer receive the worship of those who have dishonored the marriage oath. Not only that, but the passage goes on to disclose the connection between seeking a "godly offspring" and honoring the terms of the marital agreement.

The words that were exchanged on your wedding day to promise to love, cherish, and honor each other were not just part of the ceremony. They were said in the process of making your relationship a legally binding covenant under the principle of two becoming one flesh (Mark 10:6–8).The ceremonial oath you made to each other is the public display of your marriage covenant before God, just as the act of baptism is your public demonstration of entering into the new covenant with Christ.

In the same way, communion is a symbol of a renewal—or remembrance—of the oath you made at baptism. Sexual intimacy, like communion, is the revisiting of the oath made at the time of marriage—the oath declaring two individuals to now be united as one flesh.

Now, I know you've been waiting for this, because what good is a marriage guide without something to say about one of the best parts of marriage—sex. I'm glad you held on because this will be worth the wait. Sexual intimacy is far more important and far more powerful than many of us realize. Sexual intimacy is to marriage what communion is to the cross—it is a revisiting of the foundational oath of the covenant.

When a couple gets married and they become sexually

intimate, there is a sharing of life that is different from the ordinary, everyday aspects of life. The sexual union takes place at a greater spiritual level.

Typically, couples share their lives together, talk together, eat together, and all of the other things that they do together when they get married. But in sexual bonding, there is a sharing and partaking that goes deeper than just the ordinary living together. God crafted it this way, and even initiated that the first act of sexual intimacy would serve as a testimony of the marital covenant.

> SEXUAL INTIMACY, LIKE COMMUNION, IS THE REVISITING OF THE OATH MADE AT THE TIME OF MARRIAGE— THE OATH DECLARING TWO INDIVIDUALS TO NOW BE UNITED AS ONE FLESH.

This is because, most often, covenants required the shedding of blood: God would kill an animal, Christ died on the cross—a sacrifice was made somehow to enter into the relationship. God fashioned a woman the way He did so that if a woman is a virgin on her wedding night, it is normal for her to bleed—because a covenant is being established.

Sexual intimacy in marriage is usually understood only in terms of its physical dimension. Not that the physical part of sex isn't wonderful. It is. But why stop there? Sexual intimacy is a powerful force to enrich your life not only in the physical, but also in the spiritual. In fact, we learn from Paul in his letter to the Corinthians that marital sexual intimacy is a powerful tool to evoke blessings in a marriage. Married couples can even choose to abstain from sexual intimacy for a time, through a mutual agreement, in order to seek blessings from God through prayer. "Do not deprive each other except by mutual consent and for a time, so that you may devote yourselves to prayer. Then come together again" (1 Corinthians 5:6).

Sexual intimacy not only revisits the oath in a marriage relationship, but it is the ongoing expression of commitment, tenderness, and passion. One of the worst things you can do is to make ritual what is supposed to be sacred. Don't ever allow sexual intimacy, something so completely profound, to turn into something ordinary.

CONTINUITY

Underneath the overarching area of ethics and flowing out of the area of sanctions, we find what is called "continuity." Continuity refers to the transfer of an inheritance. It was God's intent when He started in the garden with Adam and Eve that the results of the marriage covenant would be passed down generationally through their offspring.

The sanctions of the covenant, blessings and curses, were not to terminate with the parents. The Bible tells us clearly in Exodus chapter 20, that the decisions of the parents can have repercussions down to the third and fourth generations. We read,

> You shall not worship them or serve them; for I, the Lord your God, am a jealous God, visiting the iniquity of the fathers on the children, on the third and the fourth generations of those who hate Me. (Exodus 20:5)

The decisions we make in our marriages can have generational repercussions, either for good or for bad, not only for our families, but also for our society. For several decades we have experienced the beginning tremors of this with the increasing number of divorces as well as the explosion of single-parent households due to couples choosing not to get married. These decisions have left us with a generation of fatherless children who display tremendous behavioral and emotional problems. Not only that, these conditions have also paved the way for the re-definition of the family unit through the call for legalization of gay marriages.

Our society reflects the stability and health of our families. Most of the negative issues facing our society can be directly traced to this breakdown of the family. Because of the discontinuity in the garden, chaos replaced calm, death replaced life, and pressure replaced peace.

When, however, we function properly under God's covenant, God transfers through us to others the blessings of the covenant promises. Continuity creates a bond between God and those who come after the immediate participants in the covenant, allowing them to take advantage of its provisions.

Marriage is a sacred covenant and not just a social contract. God promised to bless the offspring of the male and female if they faithfully functioned in accordance with His rule. Just as He committed to keep His covenant to Abraham, Isaac, and Jacob— transferring the promised inheritance through the family line—God has sanctions to transfer through us to future generations as well.

Marriage is more than just a relationship arranged for procreation or fellowship; it is a covenantal union created with the unique opportunity to allow each partner to carry out dominion not only in the current realm of influence, but also throughout history. Continuity offers the potential of leaving a lasting legacy of good throughout time, or for handing down havoc that others will have to either live in, or learn how to overcome.

A CORD OF THREE STRANDS

It is said that a "cord of three strands is not quickly torn apart" (Ecclesiastes 4:12). In marriage, we will find the ability to maintain a healthy, functioning relationship that is not headed to divorce court by recognizing this summary principle.

In a covenantal marriage, there are more than just two people entering the covenant. A husband and a wife enter into a covenant when they get married, but they enter into that covenant along with God. Just like the Trinity is made up of three coequal Persons who are One—God the Father, God the Son, and God the Holy Spirit—marriage is an earthly replica of this divine Trinity.

> ## OUR SOCIETY REFLECTS THE STABILITY AND HEALTH OF OUR FAMILIES. MOST OF THE NEGATIVE ISSUES FACING OUR SOCIETY CAN BE DIRECTLY TRACED TO THIS BREAKDOWN OF THE FAMILY.

It is important to point out that when God calls couples to oneness with each other, He is not calling them to lose their uniqueness. As revealed in the Trinity, oneness is not sameness. It is not one spouse being just like the other spouse. God's creative variety is bountiful. Each spouse has been designed with his or her distinct personality. What makes true oneness is unity of purpose—when a couple uses their differences and unique qualities in such a way as to propel them toward a common end, purpose, and vision. It is the sense that the goal that they are headed toward is bigger than their own individual preferences.

However, this depth of unity—that which creates true oneness—can only be accomplished by the Spirit of God. We are made up of body, soul, and spirit. The physical attraction, our bodies, that might have drawn two people together, if it hasn't already, will eventually fade. Our souls, because they have been distorted through our history, background, personal sin, and other people's influence on our lives, often lead to conflict at worst and relational management at best—but not oneness. But when the Holy Spirit unites with our spirits as we align ourselves under the purposes and direction of God, He makes us one. Consequently, if we are not seeking oneness through His Spirit, we limit the active role of God in our lives.

You cannot leave God at the altar and expect to have a thriving marriage. God must join you in your home, according to the aspects He has set up in His covenant: transcendence, hierarchy, and ethics. When He does, and when you abide by His authority, He can make your house a real home. You cannot do it alone. You cannot even do it as husband and wife. God must be the cord that keeps you together.

His power operating in your life is the only power that can save your life, your marriage, and your home. When Christ arose from the dead, He gave mankind access to the power of His resurrection (Romans 6:4; Philippians 3:10) and the presence of the Holy Spirit (John 14:16–18). That power and presence can enable you and your mate to live together, love each other, trust each other, and share life with each other until death parts you. God alone has given mankind the ability to do that.

God made marriage, and because He did, marriage matters. I challenge you to commit yourselves to God and function within the parameters of His divinely orchestrated covenant of marriage. Let Him remake your marriage into something that He can use not only to glorify Himself, but to enable you to exercise dominion and experience enjoyment in your life.

THE URBAN
ALTERNATIVE

THE PHILOSOPHY

D r. Tony Evans and The Urban Alternative (TUA) **equips, empowers,** and **unites** Christians to **impact** *individuals, families, churches,* and *communities* for rebuilding lives from the inside out.

We believe the core cause of the problems we face in our personal lives, homes, and societies is a spiritual one; therefore, the only way to address them is spiritually. We've tried a political, social, economic, and even a religious agenda. It's time for a Kingdom Agenda—God's visible and comprehensive rule over every area of life.

THE PURPOSE

TUA ministers to *a world in chaos* with the goal of restoring *every area of life* to its *divine order* under the rule of God. When each biblical sphere of life functions in accordance with God's Word, the net results are an evangelized and discipled people. As people learn how to govern themselves under God, they then transform the institutions of family, church, and society from a biblically based kingdom perspective.

THE PROGRAMS

To achieve our goal we use a variety of strategies, methods, and resources for reaching and equipping as many people as possible.

• *Broadcast Media*

Millions of individuals experience *The Alternative with Dr. Tony Evans* through the daily radio broadcast playing on more than **600 stations** and in more than **40 countries**. The broadcast can also be seen on several television networks, and is viewable online through the Internet at www.tonyevans.tv.

• *Leadership Training*

The Kingdom Agenda Conference *progressively develops* churches to meet the demands of the 21st century while maintaining the Gospel message and the strategic position of the church. The conference introduces *intensive seminars, workshops,* and *resources,* addressing issues affecting

> Community
> Family
> Leadership
> Organizational Health and Growth
> Ministry Programs
> Theology, Bible, and more.

Pastors' Wives Ministry, founded by Dr. Lois Evans, provides *counsel, encouragement*, and *spiritual resources* for pastors' wives as they serve with their husbands in the ministry. A primary focus of the ministry is the **First Lady Conference** that offers senior pastors' wives a safe place to *reflect, renew*, and *relax* along with training in personal development, spiritual growth, and care for their emotional and physical well-being.

The Kingdom Agenda Fellowship of Churches (KAFOC) provides a *viable network* for *like-minded pastors* who embrace the **Kingdom Agenda** philosophy. Pastors have the opportunity to *go deeper with Dr. Tony Evans* as they are given greater biblical knowledge and practical applications and resources to impact individuals, families, churches, and communities. KAFOC welcomes *senior and associate pastors* of churches regardless of size, denominational affiliation, or race.

National Church Adopt-A-School Initiative (NCAASI) prepares churches across the country to impact communities by using *public schools as the primary vehicle for effecting positive social change* in urban youth and families. Leaders of churches, school districts, and faith-based and other nonprofit organizations are equipped with the knowledge and tools to *forge partnerships* and build *strong social service delivery systems*.

• *Resource Development*

We are fostering lifelong learning partnerships with the people we serve by providing a variety of published materials. We offer books, audiotapes, videos, and booklets to strengthen people in their walk with God and ministry to others.

- *Outreach Model*

The Turn•Around Agenda (formerly Project Turn•Around)
TTA is a comprehensive church-based community impact strategy. It addresses such areas as economic development, education, housing, health revitalization, family renewal, and reconciliation. To model the success of the project, TUA invests in its own program locally. We also assist churches in tailoring the model to meet the specific needs of their communities, while simultaneously addressing the spiritual and moral frame of reference.

For more information, a catalog of Dr. Tony Evans'
ministry resources, and a complimentary copy of
Dr. Evans' devotional magazine,
call (800) 800-3222
or write TUA at P.O. Box 4000, Dallas TX 75208
or log on to TonyEvans.org